IMAGES
of America

CEDAR FALLS
IOWA

IMAGES
of America

CEDAR FALLS
IOWA

Brian C. Collins

ARCADIA

Published by Arcadia Publishing,
an imprint of Tempus Publishing, Inc.
2 Cumberland Street
Charleston, SC 29401

Printed in Great Britain.

Library of Congress Catalog Card Number: 98-87703

For all general information contact Arcadia Publishing at:
Telephone 843-853-2070
Fax 843-853-0044
E-Mail arcadia@charleston.net

For customer service and orders:
Toll-Free 1-888-313-BOOK

Visit us on the internet at http://www.arcadiaimages.com

Cover Image: Pictured is the interior of the L.O. Hieber and Company Pharmacy, which was located at 222 Main Street. This photograph of the soda fountain counter was taken about 1900. Ben Hieber is standing in the center of the picture.

CONTENTS

INTRODUCTION

The city of Cedar Falls is located in Black Hawk County, in the northeast corner of the state of Iowa. The area lies in the fertile valley of the Red Cedar River (now simply called the Cedar River), which runs diagonally through the center of the county from the northwest to the southeast.

The land that was to become Cedar Falls was originally the domain of Native Americans of the Saux and Fox tribes, who hunted and trapped along the banks of the river. The first white man to enter the area was most probably a French trapper named Gervais Paul Someneaux, who went there in 1837 to trap furs and trade with the Saux and Fox. Although Someneaux left within a year, the rich soil and abundant game in the area insured that he would not be the last white man to come.

In 1845 William Sturgis migrated to the area with his family and built the first permanent cabin near a drop in the river known as the Falls. Calling the site Sturgis Falls, he settled in and planned to develop the area with his brother-in-law Erasmus D. Adams. Both men realized the possibilities of the site for a sawmill, and set about building a brush dam to harness the river's power. They also cleared nearby plots of land in order to farm them. Within a short time their tiny community began to grow, beginning with the first white child born in the region on October 1, 1846, William Sturgis's daughter Jeanette.

When Iowa was granted statehood in 1846, more people began to join Sturgis and Adams in their settlement. Although their community was growing, the partners were hampered in their enterprise by a lack of capital. By 1847 the dam and sawmill begun by the two men was still incomplete. Seeing their difficulty, John Overman, Dempsey Overman, and John T. Barrick, new arrivals to the area, stepped in and offered to buy Sturgis's claim. Sturgis acquiesced and sold his 280 acres to the three men for $2,200.

In the spring of the following year the Overmans and Barrick moved their families to Sturgis Falls and constructed a better brush and log dam across the river. They also dug a millrace to channel the river's power to the site they had chosen for a sawmill. Within a short time they had built the first operational sawmill in the county. In 1849 Barrick and the Overmans changed the name of the community to Cedar Falls. The following year they added to their business concerns by building a gristmill. Soon other businessmen came to Cedar Falls and set up mills and factories along the river.

With industry in Cedar Falls starting to emerge, the population grew even faster. By the end of 1850, 26 families, comprising 135 persons, were living in the city. Shops began to spring up along Main Street, and the beginnings of city government started to take shape, as John Overman became the first mayor in 1851. His brother Dempsey had been elected the first postmaster two years previously.

The year 1853 saw Cedar Falls being selected as the county seat of Black Hawk County. However, the city was not to retain the title for long. The nearby city of Waterloo was growing rapidly also, and soon a rivalry sprang up over which community would better serve as the county seat. Although the people of Cedar Falls were determined that their city should continue to hold the title, the Iowa Legislature was persuaded to hold a special election in 1855 to decide which community was better suited. Unfortunately, Cedar Falls lost the election and the county seat was transferred to Waterloo. Despite this setback, the city continued to grow, and with the coming of the railroads in 1861 Cedar Falls entered a new phase of prosperity.

With the outbreak of the Civil War many Cedar Falls men went off to fight for the Union. Some of these men did not come back, leaving their families without any means of support. Following the war, a Soldiers' Orphans' Home was built to care for the children of the men who had died. Completed by 1869, the home cared for these children until they were old enough to leave. In 1876 the Orphans' Home was converted into the Iowa State Normal School, an institution set up to train school teachers. The school prospered and grew, going through several name changes as it matured (Iowa State Teacher's College, State College of Iowa, and the University of Northern Iowa). The college rapidly became an important asset to the growing community.

By the 1890s the city had become a thriving center of industry, with a population of 5,553 persons. Around this time Cedar Falls acquired the title of the "Garden City" due to its lovely tree-lined streets and well-kept homes. The city was graced with good schools, fine churches, and elegant residences, which filled the people of Cedar Falls with a deep pride in their community. The improvement of the city through public service by its citizens was a constant feature during these early years, and many prominent residents contributed to the community's betterment.

By the end of the 19th century many of the businesses that enhanced the prosperity of Cedar Falls had been founded. Raab's Stoneware and Terra Cotta Works produced all manner of ceramic products, from sewer pipes to vases; Jens Nielsen invented the pump that was later to lead to the formation of the Viking Pump Company; and Clay Equipment Company (originally the Iowa Gate Company) was started in 1899. Holst's Printing Company began operations in 1882; and Latta's School Supply was founded in 1898. Along with these, many other businesses also found a home in Cedar Falls, contributing to its lively commercial history.

The photographs in this volume depict life in Cedar Falls during the first 79 years of the city's existence. Although some of what is illustrated has long since vanished, much still remains and is cherished by its citizens. These images, from the photographic archives of the Cedar Falls Historical Society, give an excellent picture of the forces which shaped the city. They also illustrate what daily life was like for the people of Cedar Falls, from its beginnings as a frontier community in 1845 to its emergence as a modern city in 1925.

One

BEGINNINGS OF
"THE GARDEN CITY"

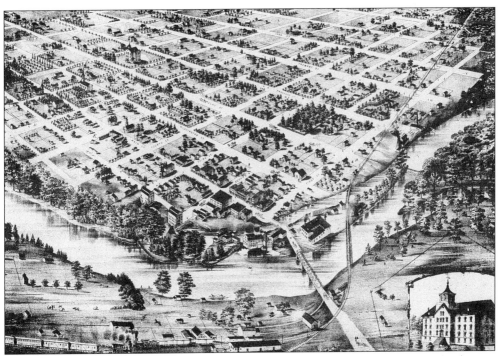

This lovely panoramic lithograph of Cedar Falls is from the year 1868. It shows how far the city had expanded 23 years after its founding by William Sturgis. By this time the city had been laid out in a neat grid pattern, with its mills clustered close to the Cedar River to take advantage of its abundant water power. The city's population in that year was approximately 1,700.

William Sturgis (1817–1901), the first permanent white settler in what became Cedar Falls, arrived in 1845 and built a double cabin near the river at what is now First and Franklin Streets. Naming the area Sturgis Falls, he laid out a claim on both sides of the Cedar River, including much of what is now downtown Cedar Falls. His daughter Jeanette was the first white child born in Black Hawk County, in 1846.

In 1853 the first schoolhouse was built in Cedar Falls, on the corner of Fifth and Main Streets. It was a frame building, 16 by 20 feet, with a belfry. The school bell was purchased with the proceeds of a festival dinner given on February 22, 1854, by the ladies of the community. Cast by the Meneeley Foundry Company of West Troy (Watervliet), New York, the bell is now in the possession of the Cedar Falls Historical Society. This building served as a school until 1863.

The Field Brothers Barn, located on Highway 57 West, was built in 1873 of local limestone. This lovely Victorian Gothic barn is the only surviving building of the estate of William and Charles Field, who were prominent early bankers in Cedar Falls. They were also importers of fine horses, cattle, hogs, and sheep, which they raised on their 3,000-acre farm. Their home was the gathering place of Cedar Falls society until the panic of 1893 cost them their fortune.

Another early limestone structure, one of the oldest surviving residential homes in Cedar Falls, is the house at 1509 Main Street, which was built around 1854. Its limestone was most likely quarried locally.

This is the northwest corner of Second and Main Street as it looked in 1875. The shop nearest the camera was A.M. Estey's Dry Goods. Next in line is F.N. Chase's grocery store, followed by an unidentified building, and fourth in line, with the balcony, is the Carter House hotel. The Carter House was originally named the Winslow House and was built in 1853. Today the Black Hawk Hotel sits on the site. Note the unpaved streets.

The Monitor House Hotel, operated by Kaynor and Son, was located on the east side of Main Street, between Fourth and Fifth Streets. This drawing dates to about 1875.

A fine example of Victorian Gothic Revival architecture is the home located at 1021 Clay Street, which can be seen in the background of this 1880 photograph. Built in 1867 by Fitzroy Sessions, the home features a scroll bargeboard, steep roof, and keystone arches over the bay windows. Mr. Sessions built the house after returning home from the Civil War, where he served as an officer in the Union Army.

John Milton Overman (1817–1906), the first mayor of Cedar Falls, came to the city in 1847 and immediately became a driving force in its commercial life. In time he became one of the wealthiest citizens in Cedar Falls. Throughout his life he encouraged the growth of the city and campaigned relentlessly for the introduction of railroads. He died at his home on West Sixth Street at the age of 92. This portrait dates to about 1865.

This lithograph of the Soldiers' Orphans' Home dates to 1875. The home was built in 1869 to house the children of Union soldiers killed in the Civil War. It was a four-story brick structure located at Twenty-third and College Streets. In 1876 the building was converted into a teachers' college known as the Iowa State Normal School. During this period the building was known as Central Hall, and was used as a classroom and office until it was destroyed by fire in 1965.

Central School occupied an entire city block bordered by Clay, Franklin, Seventh, and Eighth Streets. It was built in 1863 to replace the first schoolhouse, which was constructed in 1853, on Fifth and Main. Central School was renamed Lincoln School in the 1890s. It was a spacious three-story brick structure which served the community until 1923.

This is a view looking north over the Cedar River from the corner of First and Main Streets. In the foreground is the bridge over the millrace. Farther down is the old iron Main Street Bridge, built in 1872 at a cost of $20,000. This view was taken about 1875.

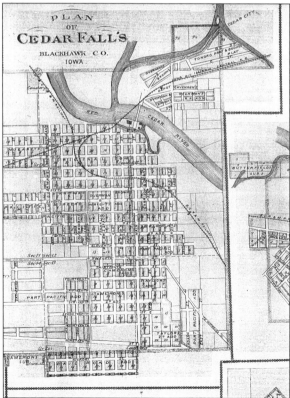

This photograph from the 1890s shows the millrace, which was located between First Street and the Cedar River. It was constructed in 1848 by John T. Barrick, John Overman, and Dempsey Overman to take advantage of the water power provided by the river. The replacement of water power with electricity in the 1920s made the millrace obsolete. In the 1970s the millrace was filled in.

This street plan of Cedar Falls from 1875 shows the expansion of the city to the south and west. It also shows the addition of a second railroad line through the city.

"Silsby" Steam power Fire Engine
made at Seneca N.Y.

The Cedar Falls Fire department assembled proudly around their new firefighting equipment. Organized in 1867 with 85 citizens enrolled, the fire department had a single Silsby Steam Fire Engine and two hose carts. By 1893 it had developed into a larger, more professional organization comprising three hose companies of 22 members each, under the direction of a fire chief.

Peter Melendy (1823–1901) came to Cedar Falls in 1856 and became one of the city's leading businessmen, as well as a devoted public servant. He was instrumental in securing the construction of the Soldiers' Orphans' Home, organizing factories, and bringing railroads to the city. He served as mayor of Cedar Falls from 1896 to 1901.

These celebrations attended the ground-breaking ceremony of the Iowa Central Railroad at Cedar Falls on September 19, 1865. Despite the enthusiasm, the Iowa Central turned out to be a disaster for its investors, and the railroad was never completed. However, railroads eventually did come to Cedar Falls, and within 30 years the Illinois Central Railroad, the Burlington, Cedar Rapids and Northern Railroad, the Cedar Falls and Minnesota Railroad, and the Chicago Great Western Railroad were all operating lines into the city.

By the end of the 1870s, dozens of shops had sprung up along Main Street. Pictured is Wilson and Williams Dry Goods, which was operated by Mr. S. Wilson and Mr. W.T. Williams. The shop specialized in selling carpets, boots, shoes, hats, caps, furnishing goods, trunks, and traveling bags. It was located in what was known as the Phoenix Block, at numbers 125 and 127 Main Street.

Pictured is the corner of Main and Fourth Streets as it looked in 1882. As can be seen in the photograph, the city had by this time acquired its characteristic wooden sidewalks, which were intended to keep pedestrians dry when the streets became seas of mud during wet weather. In the distance can be seen the spires of some of the city's churches, and in the right background can be seen the roof and bell tower of Central School, which was completed in 1863.

Two
THE CITY AT WORK

Employees in the lumberyard of the Harris and Cole Brothers Pump Works take a break to pose for the camera around 1890. The works, formed in 1873, turned out wooden pumps, as well as lumber for construction. In the background can be seen the pump factory building, which was located at the foot of Main Street near the river. This building now houses the Old Broom Factory Restaurant.

The washer-women of Harner's Steam Laundry, which was located at 116 West First Street, are shown outside the business in this 1895 view. As is evident from the photograph, it was for the most part a non-mechanical process.

A crew is shown hard at work digging the basement of the Cotton Theater, at the corner of First and Main Streets, in 1908. The crew is using a horse-drawn earth scoop (lower left corner) and a steam-powered earth mover (at top center) to clear the dirt. In the background of the photograph can be seen Harner's Steam Laundry which, judging by the condition of its sign, appears to have fallen on hard times.

Coopers of the Cedar Falls Cooperage Works show off the tools of the trade and a wagon full of their product ready for delivery. The business was started in 1876 by Michael Hammond, and by 1893, employed ten men. It was located on the corner of First and Washington Streets. This photograph was taken around 1885 in front of the nearby Russell, Goodman and Company Foundry and Machine Shop.

Employees of the Bozarth Brothers Sorghum Works were photographed in 1893. The factory was built in 1884 for $8,000. It produced about 35,000 gallons of syrup annually, with a total value of $14,000. Mr. Bozarth is in the center of the picture with his arms crossed.

This determined-looking crew of Company Number 2 of the Cedar Falls Fire Department had their picture taken about 1893. Companies 1 and 2 were located at city hall on West Third between Main and Washington Streets (which is where this photograph was taken). Company 3 was located at Eighth Street, between Clay and Franklin Streets.

This is the interior of Ed Gallagher's blacksmith shop at the Harris and Son Company Carriage Works, located at the corner of Washington and West Third Streets. Ed Gallagher is standing on the left of the photograph, which was taken about 1901.

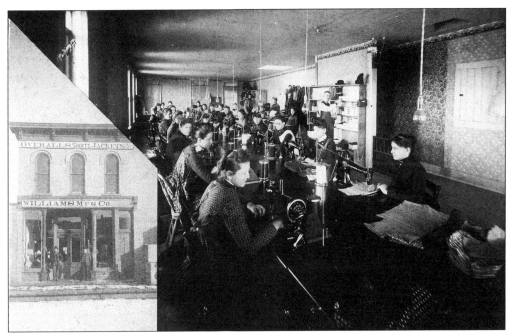

Ladies of the Williams' Manufacturing Company are hard at work over their sewing machines around 1901. Located at 120 West First Street, the company made shirts, trousers, jackets, duck coats, and overalls. It was organized by W.T. Williams in 1887 and eventually had 60 sewing machines in use daily. Of their 60 employees, the majority were women.

This is a view taken inside the offices of the Iowa Gate Company in 1910. Seated in the center of the photograph is Joseph B. Clay, the president and general manager of the firm. Seated on the right is bookkeeper George F. Wood. The company at that time was located at 120–130 East Second Street. The Iowa Gate Company later became the Clay Equipment Company.

Shown here is an interior shot of the Western Union Telegraph Office, located upstairs at 101 Main Street, in 1890. At the opening banquet for the Illinois Central Railroad in Cedar Falls, a toast was given by Platt Smith, "The four great cities of the North, Cedar Falls, Dubuque, Chicago and New York, you must have a telegraph as soon as possible." On December 9, 1863 Cedar Falls got one. Platt Smith sent the first message, "Did I not tell you so."

The interior of the Northwestern Bell Telephone office was photographed in 1924. The office was located upstairs at the rear of 303 Main Street. Note the gaslight in the center of the photograph, and the cast iron stove with long stovepipe.

Raab's Stoneware and Terra Cotta Works was located at 312 Water Street. John Raab, an immigrant from Austria, founded the works with his wife, Johanna, in 1875. He produced decorative stoneware, pottery, and chimney flues. He also produced minuscule vases painstakingly inscribed with the Lord's Prayer. Known as "Rebecca Vases," they were sent as gifts around the world to such noted personages as William Jennings Bryant, King George V of England, and Mrs. Woodrow Wilson. The photograph shows John and Johanna Raab beside their shop around 1890.

Pictured above is the carriage paint shop of the Kerr Brothers (James, George, and John), located at the rear of 116 East Third Street in 1894. The Kerr brothers were affiliated with the firm of John W. Bancroft, a carriage manufacturer and dealer, which was also located at 116 East Third Street.

This is an interior view of the post office, which was located at 121 Main Street, as it looked on February 15, 1892. The first post office in Black Hawk County was established in Cedar Falls in 1849, with Dempsey C. Overman as postmaster. The city's rapid growth is reflected in the rise of postal receipts, which went from $8.40 in 1849 to $11,196.65 in 1891.

Another shot from 1892 shows the interior of the post office from another angle. To the left of the photograph are intrepid mail carriers Charles P. Bley, William Sheerer, and Ismael Durand Corning.

Shown here is a portrait photograph of mail carrier Ismael Durand Corning with a special delivery, his son Duane, in 1891.

This is a service wagon of the Cedar Valley Telephone Company, which began service to the city about 1895. The company was located at 106 West Second Street.

The natural ice industry in Cedar Falls was big business before mechanical refrigeration became widespread. Pictured is the wood frame ice storage building of the Cedar Falls Ice Company, located on the Cedar River near First and Franklin Streets, as it looked in 1905. Every winter work crews filled this building to the ceiling with ice cut from the river. Once full, the ice would be dispensed around the city by deliverymen throughout the year. This building was destroyed by a fire on October 22, 1921.

This photograph of ice harvesting on the Cedar River about 1905 shows some of the equipment used in the operation. Also visible is the movable ramp leading to the ice house from the river. This could be raised as the level of the ice stacked inside the building rose.

The ice delivery wagon of the Cedar Falls Ice Company was photographed about 1908. Deliverymen needed to be strong, since their job occasionally required them to carry blocks of ice upstairs to second or third floors.

Following the loss of the original wood frame ice house to fire, a new hollow tile ice house was raised on the same location by the Cedar Falls Ice Company, in 1921. This building functioned as an ice house until 1934, when the company went out of business. It was then used as a livestock sales pavilion, an ice skating rink, and a boathouse. In 1975 the building was scheduled for demolition until a community effort raised $60,000 to save it. Today it is the home of the Ice House Museum of the Cedar Falls Historical Society. The photograph dates to 1923.

Cut blocks of ice are being sent up the ramp of the newly completed ice house in 1922. Veterans of this operation recalled it as being a tough job that required great stamina and the ability to withstand the icy blasts of winter wind which blew off the Cedar River.

The ice house interior would be filled to the ceiling following the winter ice harvest. The building had hollow tile walls 30 feet high, which insulated the ice and kept it cold even in mid-summer. The building had a diameter of 100 feet, and when full had a capacity of 6,000 tons of ice.

In 1904 Jens Nielsen developed an original pump design for removing seepage water from his stone quarry. His design proved so revolutionary that he acquired a patent on it. In 1911 he founded the Viking Pump Company, located at 220 East Fourth Street. Today the company is the largest private employer in Cedar Falls and sells its rotary pumps worldwide. This photograph, taken at the millrace near State Street (formerly Water Street), shows Mr. Nielsen in the center with P.C. Petersen (later company vice-president) and George Wyth (first president of the company) operating one of their pumps.

Illinois Central Railroad
Gift of Mr. and Mrs. Joe Smith
Dave Harner with raised hat.

This is the passenger train of the Illinois Central Railroad as it looked in 1880. To the left is the passenger depot, which was located across the Cedar River from the city. At that time the railroad ran six passenger trains and six freight trains into the city every day.

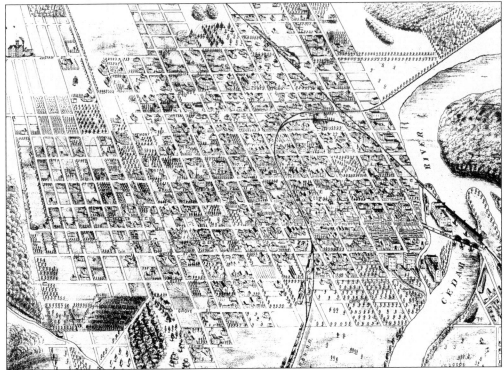

This bird's-eye view of Cedar Falls was taken in 1880. This panoramic map shows how much the city had grown since its founding 35 years earlier. By this time the residential section of the city had almost engulfed the grounds of the Iowa State Normal School (formerly the Soldiers' Orphans' Home), pictured in the upper left-hand corner.

W. W. Coombs Contractor. Cedar Falls I[...]

The work crew of the W.W. Coombs Cement Company takes a break to pose for the camera with the tools of the trade around 1908. They are paving a street somewhere in the city. The company was located at 716 West Tenth Street.

Three

MAIN STREET,
THE HEART OF THE CITY

This is the 100 block on the east side of Main Street (also known as the Phoenix Block), as it looked around the year 1880. The large edifice of the firm of Wise and Bryant Druggists, dating to 1867, is clearly visible to the right of the photograph. Aside from the Wise and Bryant building, all of these buildings are still standing, albeit in a considerably altered form.

The Burr Hotel, built in the 1870s, was located on the west side of Main Street, between First and Second Streets. The building stands on the site of the old Carter House Hotel, and was operated by two brothers, T.J. and A.N. Burr. Following the death of T.J. Burr, the hotel was purchased by a group of Cedar Falls businessmen who removed the ornamental iron balconies and renamed it the Black Hawk Hotel. This photograph dates to about 1881.

This interior shot of the Burr Hotel office was taken about 1905. A.N. Burr is behind the counter. The hotel was credited with being "a model one in neatness and is finely finished and furnished from top to cellar."

Shown here is an advertisement card for the F. Mathias Hardware Store, located on Main Street, between Second and Third Streets. Pictured is the proprietor's daughter, a less-than-happy looking Miss Lilian Mathias, wearing the company's product. This is a Lancaster Studio photograph taken in 1889.

This photograph was taken from the south end of the Main Street bridge in the 1890s. It shows the millrace bridge in the foreground and the Gibson and Burr Hotels to the right. By this time, as is evident from the photograph, the city had acquired electrical wiring.

The Townsend and Merrill Lumber and Coal Company was located on the corner of Sixth and Main Streets. This photograph, from around 1880, shows the simple facade sported by many of the early businesses in Cedar Falls. Of course, these became more elaborate as the city grew up.

This is the interior of the Cedar Falls National Bank, located at 201 Main Street, as it looked in 1898. The bank originally opened its doors on April 26, 1888, in a storeroom at 124 Main Street. In 1893 it moved to the corner of Main Street and West Second. To the left of the photograph is Roger Leavitt, who came to Cedar Falls from nearby Waterloo in 1888 to take the position of cashier for the bank.

This photograph, taken in 1893, shows the exterior of the Cedar Falls National Bank. It was located on the corner of Main and Second Streets. This building is still standing, but has lost almost all of its ornamental details.

A snowy day in 1895 is shown above. To the left is the Opera House, located at 410 Main Street, which was built in 1884 with a one thousand-person seating capacity. It was an advanced building for its time, with steam heating and electrical lighting.

This is the intersection of Main Street and Third, looking east. The Citizen National Bank in the background was founded in 1900. In 1906 Citizen National merged with the State Bank of Cedar Falls to form the Citizens Savings Bank. Note that by this time the city had brick-paved streets.

The Union Block building, which dates to 1887, is still standing at 212 and 214 Main Street. It is a wonderful example of the attractive facades which once graced Main Street.

This view of Main Street from 1917 is interesting for its wealth of now-vanished details. Note the cast iron lamppost in the foreground. To the left can be seen the trolley which once ran from Main Street to the Iowa State Teachers College. In the background is what was formerly the Burr Hotel, minus its ornamental iron balconies and renamed the Black Hawk Hotel.

This view of the millrace bridge at the north end of Main Street was taken about 1925. In the center is the Cotton Theater, which was built in 1909 to accommodate performances by touring vaudeville acts and theater troupes. Due to competition from motion picture theaters, the Cotton sold out in 1913. It became a motion picture house, the Regent Theater, in 1918. Recently the building has been restored and returned to its original function as a live-performance playhouse called the Oster-Regent Theater.

The Cedar Falls National Bank built this structure with a neo-classical facade on the corner of Main and Third Streets in 1907. This photograph dates to 1909 and apparently shows a motorcade about to get underway to advertise a cattle auction. This building is still standing but has been considerably altered.

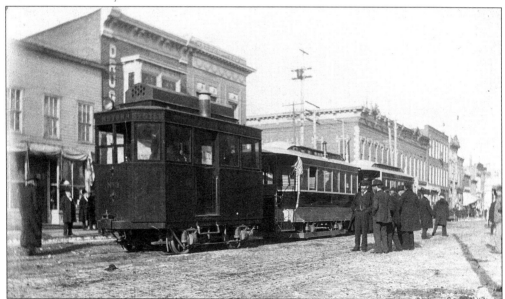

This 1897 photograph shows the newly constructed trolley line which ran from the corner of First and Main Streets to the campus of the Iowa State Normal School. The trolley was pulled by gasoline-powered Patton motor cars, and made ten round trips daily. The fare to ride the loop was 5¢.

44

The elegance of the Black Hawk Hotel is evident in this 1915 photograph, which shows waitresses in the hotel's dining room. Note the fine wood trim and the stylish wallpaper on the far wall. The Black Hawk was the successor of the Burr Hotel and continued its tradition of cleanliness and fine service.

Main Street was naturally the setting of numerous parades throughout the years. In this picture from 1900, the Shriners' float is seen being pulled by an old steam tractor past the intersection of Main and Third Streets. The Santee Brothers Real Estate, Insurance and Farm Loans establishment can be seen in the background.

This rooftop photograph is from the 1890s. To the left, with the balcony, can be seen the Sheridan Hotel (501–503 Main Street), which advertised itself as a modern hotel, lighted by electricity and heated by steam and hot air. Next to it is the First Baptist Church, which originally was a schoolhouse until purchased and remodeled by the Baptist congregation in 1860. In the distance, at the end of Main Street, can be seen the old iron bridge.

Shown here are some Cedar Falls ladies enjoying soft drinks at the soda counter of L.O. Hieber and Company Pharmacy, which was located at 222 Main Street. This photograph was taken around 1900, and shows Ben Hieber in the center behind the counter.

Construction work tries to keep pace with the growing city. This photograph, taken in 1898, shows workmen using a mule team to assist them in their labors. The men are either installing brick paving or a sewer pipe down Main Street.

The interior of the YMCA looked like this in 1896. The YMCA in Cedar Falls was located on the second floor of the Pfeiffer Building, above Pfeiffer Drug Store, at 303 Main Street. Note the sumptuous interior of this room, particularly the ornate wallpaper at the top of the walls and on the ceiling.

The elegant facade of the Citizens Savings Bank, which was located at 302 Main Street, is evident in this 1925 photograph. The bank was formed in 1906 by a merger of the State Bank of Cedar Falls and the Citizens National Bank. In 1928 the Citizens Savings Bank merged with the Security Trust and Savings Bank to form the Citizens Security Trust and Savings Bank. This building is no longer standing.

This exterior shot of the Henry Mazanti Drug Store, located at 118 Main, was taken in 1894. Mr. Mazanti is shown on the delivery wagon holding the reins. This photograph clearly shows the city's wooden sidewalks, which were raised above the level of the street on stone blocks. This was done to keep pedestrians dry during inclement weather, when the dirt streets throughout the city became a morass of mud.

The proud proprietors of the Marx Israel Clothing Store posed for the camera with their wares in 1893. The shop, which was located at 207 Main, was the oldest clothing store in operation at the time that this photograph was taken.

This is the interior of the Acme Cafe as it looked in 1916. The food establishment was located at Second and Main Streets, and was operated by Mrs. Harry Onan and Ted Shelley (seen standing behind the counter). Note the ornately-embossed tin ceiling and the brass cash register to the left.

A Fourth of July parade marches down Main Street in 1896. This shot was taken looking south at the intersection of Main and Second Streets. To the left can be seen the east side of the 300 block. Note the abundance of horse-drawn wagons.

Another parade makes its way down Main Street in 1910. This photograph was taken near the intersection of Third and Main Streets, and shows the Cedar Falls Police Department, followed closely by the city's fire department. Note the colorful awnings which used to grace the storefronts along Main Street.

Four

PLACES OF WORSHIP

This lovely little frame building, at Sixth and Clay Streets, was originally built by the Methodists in 1860 and was known as the First Methodist Church. It was sold to the Congregationalists in 1864 who enlarged it, adding the front vestibule. However, after 25 years of occupancy it was determined that a larger structure was needed, so construction of a new stone building was begun. On July 7, 1889 a final farewell service was held in the little church, before its demolition.

The Methodist Church built this second structure in 1865 at Seventh and Washington Streets. Built of brick, it cost $16,000 to construct, and was used until the congregation outgrew it in the early 1890s.

The third church built by the Methodists was this imposing structure located at Eighth and Washington Streets. Begun in 1893, it was not completed until 1895. Costing $30,000 to build, it is constructed of limestone and is 72 by 96 feet in size, with a seating capacity of one thousand persons. This photograph was taken in 1894, before the formal dedication of the church.

The First Baptist Church was organized in 1854, and originally occupied a frame building on the corner of Main and Fifth Streets. This brick structure was built in 1900, at Seventh and Washington Streets, on property which had formerly belonged to the Methodist Church. This building served the congregation until it was demolished in 1975. This photograph dates to the time of the church's dedication on December 1, 1900.

The second building occupied by the Congregational Church was completed in 1889, and was located on the corner of Clay and Sixth Streets. This beautiful stone structure had lovely memorial stained-glass windows. It served its members for 73 years until a fire destroyed it in 1959.

This interior view of the Congregational Church shows well the elegant woodwork of the 1889 structure.

This brick structure, which was located at 608 Main Street, was the original home of the First Presbyterian Church. It was begun in 1858 but not completed until 1862. The steeple housed a 1,200-pound bell which was reputed to be the first church bell heard in the Cedar Valley. The building is 41 feet wide and 62 feet long.

The Reverend James M. Phillips became the founding pastor of the First Presbyterian Church on March 18, 1855. On that date he and five other men met in the old schoolhouse, which was located on Fifth and Main Streets, to organize the founding of the church. Reverend Phillips served as pastor of the Presbyterian Church until 1860.

The elegant interior of the First Presbyterian Church is shown as it looked in 1895. The organ in the center of the photograph was the first pipe organ brought into Cedar Falls. It was donated to the church by Mr. J.T. Knapp, in memory of his wife, Mary.

This photograph shows the second building occupied by the First Presbyterian Church. Begun in 1909, it was dedicated in 1910. It is located at the corner of Ninth and Main Streets. The building contains a beautiful stained-glass window in the west wall of the auditorium, which was installed as a memorial to Mr. M.N. Dayton. Mr. Dayton had contributed the money necessary to build the structure.

This simple frame building, which was located at Ninth and Franklin Streets, was the original home of the First Evangelical Church. The church was organized in 1858. The building was constructed in 1860 for $700 and served the congregation until 1876.

The second home of the First Evangelical Church was this brick structure at Ninth and Clay Streets. It was built in 1876 at a cost of $8,000, and served as the Evangelical Church home for 40 years.

Members of the German Evangelical Association pose outside the First Evangelical Church in 1895.

In 1915 the First Evangelical Church began construction on this third structure, which was dedicated the following year. It is located at Ninth and Clay Streets, and was built at a cost of $45,000. Today it is a Mennonite church.

Calvary Baptist Church was built in 1917 at 1015 Main Street. The congregation was organized in 1878, and used the facilities of the First Baptist Church until it was able to build a separate structure in 1882. Although that building was remodeled and enlarged, the congregation had outgrown it by 1917. The church then built the above structure on the same site. The photograph shows the church in 1925.

Danish Bethlehem Church,
Cedar Falls, Iowa.

On July 1, 1897, a group of Cedar Falls citizens met to organize a new Lutheran church. They drafted a constitution and chose the name Bethlehem Congregation for their church. They also laid plans for the erection of a church building. The Bethlehem Lutheran Church was completed the following year, and was a simple frame building located at the corner of Main and Fourteenth Streets. This structure was used until 1902, when a new church was built.

The interior of the Bethlehem Lutheran Church shows the simple but graceful elegance to be found in this building. Reverend Adam Dan, the first pastor of the church, wrote: "We know that there are larger and more beautiful churches, but it is only a relatively small group that has put shoulders to the task. Nevertheless the church is beautiful, especially the interior." This photograph was taken in 1898, shortly after the completion of the church.

Reverend Adam Dan was photographed sitting amid the first class to be formally confirmed in the Bethlehem Lutheran Church on March 26, 1899. The children, from left to right, are: Elizabeth Rasmussen, Margrethe Madsen, Else Christensen, Inga Nielsen, Emil Petersen, Hans P. Hansen, Albert Rasmusen, Mattie Petersen, Chris Christensen, and Alma Petersen.

In 1867 the First German Evangelical Lutheran Church was organized, and began construction on this simple frame building known as St. John's Church. It was located at the corner of Tremont and West Eighth Streets. By 1913 the congregation had outgrown this building and plans were laid to erect a new structure at Eighth and College Streets. The photograph was taken in February 1915, shortly before the church was demolished.

The Nazareth Danish Lutheran Church was completed in 1873 on the corner of Ninth and Bluff Streets. Prior to the construction of this church, the congregation used the German Lutheran Church at Tremont and Eighth Streets. Nazareth Lutheran Church served its congregation for more than 30 years until it was replaced by a larger structure built on the same site in 1911. This photograph was taken in 1880.

The congregation of the Nazareth Danish Lutheran Church poses for a photograph outside the building in 1895. At this time, conflict had developed within the membership of the church, which led to 50 members of the congregation withdrawing and forming the Bethlehem Lutheran Church in 1897.

In 1911 the Nazareth Danish Lutheran Church built this new brick structure on the site of its original church at Ninth and Bluff Streets. It served the congregation until 1962, when a larger building was constructed at Twenty-seventh and Main Streets.

St. Luke's Episcopal Church, located at Seventh and Main Streets, was completed in 1868. It was a simple frame structure which was covered with stucco in the early 1920s. St. Luke's parish was organized in 1855, and used the old school building located on Fifth and Main Streets until this building was completed. It served its members until 1965, when it was demolished to make way for an office building. This photograph was taken in 1925.

Saint Patrick's Catholic Church was organized in 1854. The following year the congregation built a small brick structure on the corner of Eighth and Washington Streets. It served the Catholic community until it was torn down to make room for this larger building, which was completed in 1876. Measuring 40 by 100 feet, this structure cost $12,000 to build. This building served as the Catholic church until it was gutted by fire in 1913. The photograph dates to around 1908.

The third incarnation of Saint Patrick's Catholic Church was built on the site of the previous Saint Patrick's, at Eighth and Washington Streets. This fine brick structure was built at a cost of $55,000. The cornerstone was laid by Archbishop J. Keane in October 1915. It was formally dedicated on June 6, 1916.

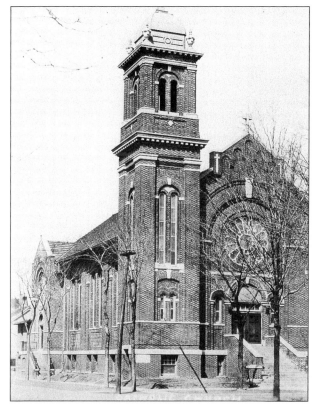

Saint Patrick's Parochial School, on Seventh and Washington Streets, was completed in 1891 for $1,083. It served the parish as both a school and as a home for the Sisters of Charity. The wood-frame building was demolished in 1951 to make room for a new structure.

Riverview Park Evangelical Grounds was established by the Evangelical Church in 1916 as the site for its annual camp meeting. The following year a tabernacle, administration building, dormitory, kitchen, and dining hall were built to accommodate worshippers attending the annual retreat. Eventually 85 cabins were also constructed. Since 1922 the park has been the site of the annual one-week Cedar Falls Bible Conference, an inter-denominational gathering that has earned national recognition.

Five

ELEGANT PRIVATE HOMES

This etching from 1875 shows the home of Dempsey C. Overman, which was located on Twelfth Street, between Walnut and Olive Streets. This Italianate-style home was built in the 1860s.

Dempsey C. Overman (1820–1874) came to Cedar Falls in 1847, and immediately became a driving force in business and politics. With his brother he bought out the claim of William Sturgis and transformed it into a viable operation, building a dam to harness the river's power, digging the millrace, and founding factories. Much of the prosperity that Cedar Falls experienced in its early days is largely due to the efforts of the Overman brothers.

The Sawyer House, at 503 West Twelfth Street, is an example of the Queen Anne style. It was built in 1894 and features a pent-roof for each gable end, shaped porch balusters, and a multiple gable arrangement. Mr. M.W. Sawyer, the original owner, came to Cedar Falls in 1852 and operated a clothing store in the city until his death in 1918.

This is an aerial view of the Litchfield Mansion, which was built in 1922 by Edgar C. Litchfield, a wealthy manufacturer. The mansion is located at 1603 Mandalay Drive. It was built at a cost of $400,000 and had 56 rooms which included a shooting gallery, gymnasium, bowling alley, and billiards room. The Litchfields lost their home during the Depression, and it was subsequently turned into a restaurant and nightclub, an inn, and finally an apartment house.

The Rownd House was constructed in 1865 by Samuel H. Rownd Sr. It was built of local limestone in the Queen Anne style. The two-story house has four bedrooms with oak woodwork throughout. Mr. Rownd came to Cedar Falls in 1850, and within a few years had acquired nearly 4,000 acres of land. The house is located at 4119 South Main Street.

This home, located at 415 Walnut Street, was built by T.L. French in 1874, in the Italianate style. It featured five coal-burning fireplaces of Italian marble, 12-foot ceilings decorated with plaster cast medallions, and woodwork of Norway pine and black walnut. In 1886 it was purchased from Mr. French by John Forrest, a local mill owner. It became the home of Andrew Dicken in 1909, and finally passed to Alonzo Gleason in 1933.

This Queen Anne-style home, located at 519 Washington Street, was built in 1865 by Rutledge Harris. The house features unique variations in its siding, which includes an open or half-timbered appearance, highly decorated corbels, and slightly hipped roof gable ends. The woodwork on the first floor is cherry, and the outside ornaments were made by the Harris and Cole Brothers Works in Cedar Falls.

In 1891 Norman Henry Harris built this home at 601 West Twelfth Street. It is a Queen Anne-style structure with Gothic influences. The third floor contained a ballroom with space for an orchestra located in the tower. Mr. Harris was the co-owner of Harris and Cole Brothers Works in Cedar Falls, which manufactured wooden water pumps. The company also made gables, porches, and stairways, some of which were no doubt incorporated in this building.

This photograph, from the 1890s, shows the Queen Anne-style house which was the home of Mr. Edward A. Snyder, the editor of the *Cedar Falls Gazette*. The home was located at 1219 Washington Street. The house was an excellent example of the elegant private homes which used to dot the city. Unfortunately, this home is no longer standing.

This Italianate-style home, built in 1867, is known as the Knapp/Townsend House. Banking partners J.R. Knapp and Edward Townsend constructed this home and lived in it with their wives. Tragically, the wives died within a year of each other and the banking partners split up. Edward Townsend moved out in 1878. J.R. Knapp stayed in the house until he lost his banking firm in the Depression of the 1890s. The home is located at 224 West Third Street and is now the home of the Cedar Falls Women's Club.

This is the Townsend House as it looked in 1890. This house, located at 1017 Washington Street, was built by Edward Townsend in 1878, after the death of his first wife. It is of the Italianate style with Gothic influences. The house is unique for its 11-foot ceilings, parquet floors, fireplaces in most rooms, and 19th-century intercom system from the maid's quarters to the master bedroom.

The stone quarry of Jens Nielsen, which was located at Main and Nineteenth Streets, was the source for much of the building stone used in early Cedar Falls homes. Flooding in this quarry inspired Mr. Nielsen to invent a revolutionary new kind of rotary pump that he was to patent and produce. Ultimately the pump manufacturing venture proved to be more lucrative than the quarry, becoming the Viking Pump Company in 1911. This photograph was taken in 1893.

Shown above is an ice delivery to the Daniel Wild House at 501 West First Street in 1909. This large Queen Anne-style home was built around 1875 by W.A. Robinson. It features an elaborate gable arrangement, ridge line decoration, and a range of texture changes in the siding.

Perhaps the most beautiful surviving 19th-century home in Cedar Falls is the Sartori House, located at 603 Clay Street. It was built by Joseph Sartori in the late 1860s, and is a late Gothic Revival style with Italianate influences. The decorative arches above the windows are sheet iron. Mr. Sartori was an immigrant from Germany who came to Cedar Falls in the 1850s. He became a successful contractor and real estate investor, and at his death left $25,000 for the construction of Sartori Hospital.

The A.E. Lunn House, located at 1001 Washington Street, was built in 1910. It is an example of the large but less ornate family homes which were being built in the city as the Victorian era was coming to a close.

The first home of Peter Melendy, at 1107 Washington Street, was built in 1875. It is of the Italianate style and has two living rooms, two bedrooms, and one dining room. Melendy was a mayor of Cedar Falls, as well as being a moving force in business and in the establishment of the Soldiers' Orphans' Home. He also wrote one of the early histories of Cedar Falls, the *Historical Record of Cedar Falls*, in 1893.

This 1875 etching shows the well-ordered home of John Milton Overman, the first mayor of Cedar Falls. It was located at the west end of Sixth Street and was probably built shortly before this view was made. In was situated on a large plot of land with extensive gardens. The house appears to have been in the Italianate style, with a belvedere atop the roof.

The Barnum/Bryant House, at 303 Clay Street, was built in the Italianate style in 1863 by building contractor Azel D. Barnum, who also built the Soldiers' Orphans' Home. In 1874 Walter A. Bryant purchased the house and lived in it with his family until his death in 1917. The building is now one of the museums of the Cedar Falls Historical Society, a nonprofit corporation dedicated to preserving local history, which was formed in 1962.

Walter A. Bryant and his wife Cornelia were photographed near the side porch of the Barnum/Bryant House about 1910. Mr. Bryant came to Cedar Falls in 1878 and organized the Bryant-Neeley Lumber Company. He became a successful businessman, eventually expanding into other businesses under the name of W.A. Bryant and Sons. He died in his home on November 13, 1917. His wife Cornelia survived him by 13 years. They had five sons: Walter Jr., James, Philip, LeRoy, and Frank.

This is one of the homes that belonged to local historian Roger Leavitt. It is located at 1022 Washington Street. Mr. Leavitt built this home in 1889 and sold it eight years later for $3,000.

The Sheldon Fox House was built in 1863 and is Italianate in design. It is located at 402 West Second Street and originally featured 14-foot ceilings, a belvedere, and a wraparound porch. Although the building has been considerably altered, it still retains its charm.

The George Wyth House, located at 303 Franklin Street, was built in 1907 by F.W. Paulger. George Wyth, president of the Viking Pump Company, purchased the house in 1925 and added a brick outer shell to the frame structure to insulate the building. Today it is one of the house museums of the Cedar Falls Historical Society, and also contains the Viking Pump Museum, which chronicles the history of the Viking Pump Company.

George and Dorothy Wyth pose together in this 1922 photograph. Dorothy inherited the George Wyth House following the death of her father in 1955. Prior to her own death in 1979 she left the house, and a cash endowment for its maintenance, to the Cedar Falls Historical Society. After considerable restoration work, the Society opened the George Wyth Home and Viking Pump Museum to the public on December 4, 1983.

Six

INSTITUTIONS,
COLLEGES, AND SCHOOLS

Old Central School was constructed in 1863 to serve primary through high school grades. This large building occupied an entire city block, and was bordered by Seventh, Eighth, Clay, and Franklin Streets. It was known as Central School until the 1890s, when the name was changed to Lincoln School. In 1875, as the population of the city grew, a west wing was added to accommodate more students. This photograph dates to the 1870s.

Lincoln School (old Central School) was photographed in 1893 after major alterations. An east wing had been added as well as a large bell tower. This renovated building was used until 1924, when a new Lincoln School building was constructed across the street. The site on which it stood is now the school playground.

Jefferson School, also known as West School, was located on Walnut Street, between Sixth and Seventh Streets. It was built in 1864, and served both primary and high school grades. It was demolished in 1924, following the completion of the new Lincoln School.

The Cedar Falls High School was located on Main Street, between Twelfth and Thirteenth Streets. It was constructed in 1900, and was the first separate high school in Cedar Falls. This view was taken about 1906.

The Cedar Falls High School was photographed following the completion of an addition to the rear of the original structure in 1914. This building was used until 1953.

NEW LINCOLN SCHOOL BLDG

This is the new Lincoln School as it looked shortly after its construction in 1924. This building occupies an entire city block and is bordered by Franklin, Tremont, Seventh, and Eighth Streets. It was built to replace the original Lincoln School building, which was constructed in 1863. This building still serves the Cedar Falls community.

Greenwood Cemetery is located at the north end of College Street. It was begun as a family burial ground by early pioneers coming to Cedar Falls. The earliest burials belong to members of the Overman family and date to 1851. This photograph of the front gate was taken about 1908.

The Soldier's Memorial in Greenwood Cemetery was dedicated on June 14, 1914, in honor of area men who died in battle. It was erected by the Greenwood Cemetery Association. The inscription reads "In memory of our soldiers dead."

Sartori Memorial Hospital was completed in 1915 with a bequest left by Joseph Sartori Sr. Mr. Sartori, a German immigrant, was a successful contractor and real estate investor who came to Cedar Falls in the late 1850s. Upon his death he left $25,000 to the city for the construction of this building. It is located at Sixth and College Streets.

The Western Old Peoples Home, located at Tenth and Irving Streets, was built in 1911, following a gift of $20,000 from the Pfeiffer family. From the beginning the home was under the supervision of the Evangelical Church, formally coming under the ownership of the church in 1922. In 1928 the Pfeiffers donated another $60,000 for the erection of an addition, which was completed the following year.

The Carnegie-Dayton Public Library was constructed in 1902, on the corner of Main and Sixth Streets. The land on which it was built was donated to the city by Mr. and Mrs. Martin N. Dayton. The building has been greatly modified but still serves as the city library.

This is an 1880 photograph of Old Central, which was located at Twenty-third and College Streets. Originally a home for the orphans of soldiers killed in the Civil War, it became the nucleus for the Iowa State Normal School in 1876, where it was known as Old Central Hall. It served as classrooms and office space until July 22, 1965, when a fire destroyed the building. The Iowa State Normal School later became the Iowa State Teachers College, the State College of Iowa, and finally the University of Northern Iowa.

As the attendance at the college grew, new buildings were added. This photograph shows South Hall, which was built in 1882 at a cost of $35,000. In 1915 the name was changed to Gilchrist Hall, in honor of the first principal of the institution, James C. Gilchrist. The building was destroyed by fire on May 12, 1972.

In 1895 the college embarked upon the construction of its second new building. Central Hall, later called the Old Administration Building, was completed under the supervision of Resident Director Edward Townsend. The photograph above was taken in 1912.

This photograph, from 1896, shows the cluster of buildings which originally made up the campus of what was at that time called the Iowa State Normal School. They are, from left to right: South Hall (built in 1882), the Old Administration Building (built in 1895), Old Central Hall (built in 1869), and the Chapel, which dates to 1871.

This photograph, also from 1896, shows the original President's Cottage on the right. The cottage was built in 1890. Today it is one of the few surviving early structures on campus. Originally built to house the president of the college and his family, it now serves as the Ethnic Minorities Cultural and Educational Center.

In this 1896 photograph, military cadets can be seen drilling behind South Hall. In 1889, 51 students of the college petitioned the Board of Directors for instruction in military drill. Their request was granted, and eventually all male students were required to take military drill unless excused by the president of the college. Despite this, instruction in military drill proved short-lived and was soon eclipsed by athletics.

The Science Laboratory was completed in 1907. It contained classrooms, laboratories, and lecture halls for the instruction of various scientific disciplines. This photograph was taken shortly after its completion.

The auditorium was built at a cost of $100,000. Its dedication on January 30, 1902, was attended by state officials and the General Assembly.

The two cannons, located in front of the auditorium in this 1901 photograph, were presented to the college through the efforts of Congressman D.B. Henderson. They were originally brought to North America by the Spaniard, Pedro Menedez d'Aviles in 1565 for the defense of Spain's Florida colony. In 1819 the cannons, along with Florida, became the property of the federal government. The U.S. government passed them along to the college in 1901.

This is a souvenir postcard showing the faculty of the Iowa State Normal School in 1908. In the center of the photograph is Homer H. Seerley, who was president of the college from 1886 to 1928. Seerley was chiefly responsible for the rapid growth of the college in its early years.

The Training School of the college was built in 1914. It educated student teachers in realistic school settings, using real students from kindergarten through high school. The building contained 80 rooms for instruction, an assembly hall, and a library.

The college library was opened in 1911 with a collection of 30,000 volumes. It also housed a museum on the upper floor containing exhibits and specimens useful in teaching natural science. In addition, there were laboratories for instruction in mineralogy, taxidermy, and other sciences.

This is the Great Reading Room of the library as it looked in 1925. The murals on the walls were painted by William De Leftwich Dodge, who painted them in his studio in New York City. They were then brought to Cedar Falls in sections and installed in the building in the years 1920 and 1921.

The gymnasium was completed in 1905. This four-story building contains a swimming pool as well as lockers, showers, exercise rooms, classrooms, and a running track. The building cost $100,000 to construct. This 1909 view of the gymnasium shows the tennis courts being used by very conservatively dressed tennis players.

The second President's Cottage was built in 1909 to replace the original 1890 structure. It housed the president of the college and his family. The structure has been altered considerably since it was built. This photograph was taken in 1925.

An aerial view of the Iowa State Teachers College taken in 1925 shows the expansion of the college since its beginnings. Starting with one building in 1876, the institution had grown to include over a dozen structures by the time that this photograph was taken.

Seven

RECREATION AND LEISURE

Members of the Cedar Falls Municipal Band are on the march in an unidentified city in the year 1900. The band was organized in 1891 as a completely volunteer organization. It achieved a statewide reputation as the "Convention Band" and attended numerous national and state conventions as the official band of the state of Iowa. It has been in continuous existence since its inception.

This photograph shows a street fair at the intersection of Third and Main Streets in the year 1900. The colorful facade of the Zoological Eden Animal Circus no doubt attracted many visitors. In the background can be seen the newly completed Citizens National Bank.

Harry Neuman and Florence Clay were out courting on a fine spring day in 1895. This photograph was taken in front of the Clay residence at 815 Main Street. The back of the photograph contains the message that after this picture was taken the horse was startled and ran away, throwing them both out of the carriage. This no doubt put an abrupt end to their date.

Here, the family of J.M. Overman are enjoying a fine summer day outside the Overman residence. This photograph was taken on July 30, 1889, and shows the family engaged in a variety of leisure activities. In the center of the photograph, in the rocking chair, is Mr. Overman himself.

The Cedar Falls Tigers pose for the camera in 1908. This photograph is a good illustration of how much football equipment has changed in 90 years.

On October 16, 1899, President William McKinley (in center with top hat) visited Cedar Falls. Six thousand residents of the city turned out in the early morning hours to greet his train and catch a glimpse of the President.

This is a close-up photograph of President McKinley addressing the citizens of Cedar Falls. With the President were Secretary of the Treasury Lyman Gage, Secretary of the Interior Ethan A. Hancock, Secretary of Agriculture James Wilson, and Governor of the State of Iowa Leslie M. Shaw.

A very public wedding ceremony took place on Main Street in 1907, during the Merchants Carnival. This photograph appears to have been taken at the intersection of Third and Main Streets.

This aerial view shows the Cedar Valley Fairgrounds in the early 1920s. It was located east of Main Street on Seerly Boulevard. The 80-acre site was purchased by the Cedar Valley Agricultural Society in 1861. The property was later acquired by Dr. William Pettit, who renamed it the South Park Trotting Track and added a grandstand, stables, judging stand, and a half-mile race track. The area fell into disuse after 1928 when a flood destroyed Dry Run Bridge, the only access to the site.

The Cedar Falls Drum Corps pose for a studio portrait in 1885. The backdrop is a drawing of Main Street as it looked at that time.

Author Bess Streeter Aldrich (1881–1954) was born and raised in Cedar Falls. She wrote 13 novels and 160 short stories during her writing career. The house she lived in was located at 809 Franklin Street. Of this house she wrote: "Our home in Cedar Falls, Iowa, was plain and comfortable. It had started out to be a white-painted, white-shuttered type of eastern wing-and-ell house, but in my time, additional bedrooms had been built onto and atop it, so that its design was no longer catalogued in any architectural books."

A Fourth of July parade makes its way down Main Street in 1896. This was taken near the 400 block, and shows the now vanished Opera House on the right-hand side of the street. Note the restaurant window in the lower left-hand corner, which advertises dinner for 25¢.

A group of Iowa State Teachers College students went out for a drive with a four-footed friend around 1902.

Bathers are enjoying the water at Island Park in 1925. The park was the largest in Cedar Falls at that time, and comprised 104 acres situated on the north bank of the Cedar River. In the background can be seen the Bath House, which was a very modern facility for its time, with lockers, showers, and dressing rooms. The swimming area had a large natural sandy beach complete with diving towers, platforms, and slides.

This unusual family portrait was taken around 1902. Despite a great deal of research, I was unable to discover the significance of the goat with the Cedar Falls banner. However, this photographer's prop would continue to pop up again and again among photographs of Cedar Falls.

Roger Leavitt (1866–1949) was known as the unofficial historian of Cedar Falls. From an early age he began keeping scrapbook memoirs of local history, and after retiring from banking used these as the basis for a history of Cedar Falls entitled *When Cedar Falls Was Young*, published in 1928. Mr. Leavitt's scrapbooks and published works were responsible for preserving much of the city's early history.

The Push of Cedar Falls were a group of civic-minded citizens who banded together in 1880 to promote business and social activities in Cedar Falls. This photograph was taken in 1901 and features most of the city's prominent businessmen.

The natural spring at Pfeiffer Spring Park was the source of the city's water supply until the outbreak of a typhoid epidemic was blamed on it in 1911. In 1921 the spring and 10 acres of surrounding land were given to the city by the Pfeiffer family. For several years the park was a popular picnic area until settling of the ground underneath the park stopped the flow of the spring. The park is located at Grand Boulevard and Gibson Street. This photograph was taken in 1925.

Pictured above is the same goat, same wagon, same banner, different people. A group of Cedar Falls football players pose with perhaps the most photographed goat in Iowa.

Summer bathers enjoy the sand at the bathing beach in Island Park in 1925. At the time of this photograph, Cedar Falls boasted 250 acres of improved park area, having approximately 1 acre of park for every 30 people. There were ten different parks within the city ranging from 1 to 104 acres.

A citizen of Cedar Falls enjoys a Sunday drive on Main Street in 1890. For many years after the introduction of automobiles, wagons continued to be a significant mode of transportation within the city.

Another portrait photograph of our familiar friend with two young residents of the city was taken around 1902.

Shown here is a portrait of Roy and Tony Bryant in front of the Barnum/Bryant House at 308 West Third Street. This photograph was taken in front of the house in 1885, and shows the original shape of the front entrance, which has been considerably modified since this photograph was taken. The Barnum/Bryant house is now known as the Victorian Home and Carriage House Museum and is one of the museums of the Cedar Falls Historical Society.

Eight

LIFE ALONG
THE CEDAR RIVER

A photograph taken about 1924 shows a boating party on the banks of the Cedar River. The river has always been both a source of pleasure as well as danger to the city of Cedar Falls. It provided the motive power for much of the city's early industry, but periodically overflowed its banks and flooded Cedar Falls. In later years, as the importance of water power waned, it became the city's prime recreational attraction.

This image from a stereoscopic card is one of the earliest views of the Cedar River. It was produced by local photographer C.B. Melendy about 1875. The tall woman in white is most probably the photographer's wife, enjoying a leisurely stroll along the riverbank with friends.

One of the early industries that depended on the Cedar River as a source of power was the Dayton Mill, which was built in 1871. Located between the river and the millrace, it was a five-story frame structure, 60 by 60 feet in size, with a three-story frame addition 50 by 36 feet. In its prime, the mill ground 250 barrels of flour per day. This photograph probably dates to the 1890s.

This photograph from the 1890s shows the temporary dam built over the entry of the millrace to allow the installation of new head gates. In the right background can be seen the falls, which gave the city its name.

Workers are shown installing new head gates for the millrace. The men in the photograph are identified as mill workers who were put to work on this project while the mills were shut down for the installation of the head gates.

This is the dam over the Cedar River at Cedar Falls. The first dam built to provide the drop necessary to harness the river's power was begun in 1845 by William Sturgis. It was completed by the Overman brothers in 1848. The dam in this photograph dates to 1855, and served the city's industry well for a number of years.

This peaceful-looking shot of one of the city's mills was taken from the millrace around the turn of the century. The millrace was 70 feet in width and 6 feet deep.

This 1910 photograph was taken from the Main Street bridge, looking east down the river. As can be seen, the banks of the river were still heavily wooded. To the right is the old Dayton Mill.

This 1920s photograph was taken looking north across the river. In the center is the Main Street bridge. To the left is the Kleen Kwick Washing Machine Company building. This structure was originally built in 1862 for the manufacture of cornstarch. It was later used for the manufacture of wooden pumps, washing machines, and finally brooms and pickles. The building now houses the Old Broom Factory Restaurant, a popular Cedar Falls eating establishment.

Although most often a blessing to the city, the Cedar River can occasionally be a curse, especially when it overflows its banks and floods the city. This photograph was taken on April 7, 1888, after such an occurrence. It was taken just south of the Chicago Great Western Railroad Depot, at the east end of Fifth Street. In the center can be seen the depot. Just past it are the city's mills.

Miner's Mill was built by Overman and Company in 1856 for the grinding of flour. It had a capacity of 275 barrels a day. The mill had a boiler and engine house attached to it, with a 100-horsepower engine within to operate the machinery in case of low water. This photograph was taken during the flood of 1888.

This photograph was taken from across the river in 1888. The flood seems to have collapsed part of the Harris and Cole Bros. Pump Works. Damage caused by the occasional flooding of the Cedar River has been very costly to the citizens of Cedar Falls through the years.

These citizens of Cedar Falls seem undeterred from their boating expedition, despite the flooding of the city. Or maybe this was simply the easiest way to get around Cedar Falls during the flood. This shot was taken looking north from the cattle yard of the Burlington, Cedar Rapids and Northern Railroad in 1888.

Although the flooding of the river could be a catastrophe for industry, its opposite could shut down the mills as well. This photograph records one such occurrence, when the river fell way below its usual level in the mid-1880s.

This is the Main Street bridge as it looked in 1908. Beyond it can be seen the Illinois Central Railroad bridge.

The Illinois Central Railroad bridge over the Cedar River was photographed around 1908.

A very self-satisfied-looking group of gentlemen are shown at the dedication of the Illinois Central Railroad bridge in the 1890s.

A group of weekend strollers enjoys a stop near the dam on the river in the 1890s. They are standing upon the old wooden bulkhead, which was replaced in the 20th century with a concrete bulkhead.

Members of the Lenox Club enjoy an outing on the Cedar River in 1908. The club had its own houseboat which made regular excursions on the river. In an effort to protect the chastity of her charges, the dean of women students at the Iowa State Teachers College once proclaimed that female pupils were forbidden to take rides on this boat, since men were also aboard.

This flood of the Cedar River in the 1920s engulfed the Viking Pump Company building (on the right hand side of the photograph) at 220 East Fourth Street. This structure was built in 1912, shortly after the founding of the company.

A child enjoys a leisurely float on the Cedar River around 1908 in his flag-bedecked and canopied pleasure craft. Despite the river's ups and downs, it continued to be the primary recreation spot in the Cedar Valley.

This photograph shows summer cottages on the Cedar River in 1910. The city's location on the river ensured that it would always be an important vacation spot, and many vacation cottages were built along its banks throughout the years.

This view of the curve of the Cedar River from Rownd's Bluffs looking west was taken in 1908. To the left of the photograph can be seen the tracks of the Burlington, Cedar Rapids and Northern Railroad.

This view from 1922 shows the rear of the head gates that were placed at the entrance of the millrace to control the flow of water. The Overman brothers built the original head gates in 1848, and they were periodically modernized until the millrace was filled in during the 1970s.

The flood of March 21, 1897 almost completely engulfed the track crossing of the Burlington, Cedar Rapids and Northern and the Chicago Great Western Railroads. Trains stopped moving altogether until the waters receded a few days later.

Another shot from March 21, 1897 shows North Main Street completely under water. When floods such as this engulfed farms it often caused the loss of entire crops.

This photograph of the old iron Main Street bridge was taken from across the river. To the left can be seen the Dayton Mill. To the right of the center can be seen the Burr Hotel. This photograph was taken in 1897.

ACKNOWLEDGMENTS

I would like to thank the following individuals and institutions for their assistance in the creation of this book. In many instances, their support of this project has been a tremendous help, and I appreciate their continued interest:

Valerie Collins (my patient wife), the Cedar Falls Historical Society, Lynn Nielsen, Sue Lehman, Gene Lehman, Kristen Johnson Stalling (director of education for the Cedar Falls Historical Society), Saul Diamond (a longtime resident of the city and member of the Cedar Falls Historical Society), and Patrick Catel (my editor).

I would also like to acknowledge that all of the photographs in this work are from the archives of the Cedar Falls Historical Society, a nonprofit organization founded in 1962 to preserve local history. The Society operates five museums: The Victorian Home & Carriage House Museum, The George Wyth Home & Viking Pump Museum, The Little Red Schoolhouse Museum, The Ice House Museum, and the Behrens-Rapp Service Station Museum.